Copyright © 2019 by Debbie Centeno

All rights reserved. No part of this publication may be reproduced, distributed, or transmitted in any form or by any means, including photocopying, recording, or other electronic or mechanical methods, without the prior written permission of the publisher, except in the case of brief quotations embodied in critical reviews and certain other noncommercial uses permitted by copyright law. For permission requests, write to the publisher, addressed "Attention: Permissions Coordinator," at the address below.

Debbie Centeno
debbie413@gmail.com

Printed in the United States of America

Make An Extra Income While You Mystery Shop

by

Debbie Centeno

TABLE OF CONTENT

What Is A Mystery Shopper?	2
Is Mystery Shopping for Me?	4
What's Expected From Me?	6
No Special Equipment Needed	9
Preparing to Shop	10
Keeping Track of Your Shops	12
Is It Worth My Time?	13
Reliable Companies	15
Where Do I Begin	20
A Little Extra	23
About the Author	24

What Is A Mystery Shopper?

Companies use mystery shopping to evaluate if the company's standards are being met. They want to know in what areas they need to improve to offer the best customer experience ever. They also use this method to evaluate their employees thus allowing them to offer incentives and promotions to good employees. Therefore, they hire people, through a third-party, to visit their store as a regular consumer and give feedback to the company. For that, they compensate and/or reimburse you for any expenses incurred.

There are many companies out there which recruit mystery shoppers for pay. You are not hired as an employee but as an independent contractor. This means you will get a Form 1099-M for tax purposes if you made $600 total or more for the year in any one company. Some of the companies will just reimburse your expenses such as restaurants, cafés, and pubs. But that's okay too. Everyone eats out or enjoys a cold beer once in a while, so why not do it for free?

You do not need to stick to one company alone. You can sign up to as many as you want. I have over ten companies I do shops for; which I will provide to you in this book further on. There are many more than what I will provide, however, I have not worked for all of them. Therefore, I will give you the names of those that I have experience with. There was a time where I did shops for over twenty companies. But some have closed their doors and many have merged with others.

Let it be known there is NO CHARGE to become a mystery or secret shopper. None of the companies that I've contracted with has asked for registration fees or any type of fees. You register for free, do the shop and get paid, that's it.

Is Mystery Shopping for Me?

I do Mystery Shopping or Secret Shopping, (however you wish to call it) as a hobby. It's not something I just began. I've been a mystery shopper since 2005. I shop at grocery stores, department stores, convenience stores, gasoline stations, apartment complex, banks, entertainment, and amusement parks, restaurants, fitness centers, cell phone shops, travel, and so many others.

There are many perks to being a mystery shopper. You choose where you want to shop, the time and dates available. You can do as little as one shop per day or as many as three or four or whatever you feel comfortable with. Of course, it's depending on the type of shop, place, and your will to complete them.

Mystery Shopping is not a get rich quick scheme and I'm not sure someone can make a living out of it. I know I can't but there may be some people who do it. It is enjoyable and while we make a few bucks here and there, we are also contributing to a higher quality of customer service for the consumer. One small suggestion though, just because we're evaluating a business does not give us the right to disrespect the staff or cause any problems at the establishment. We are here to see and document with total respect for all parties involved.

What's Expected From Me?

Let me make it clear though, mystery shopping is not for everyone. There are important factors to keep in mind to be a good shopper. First and foremost, shopping is not the beginning, nor the end of it. Once you schedule the shop, you have to make sure you read the scenario provided and follow all the steps necessary for a successful shop. Your pay depends on how you performed the shop and if you followed instructions.

A good mystery shopper will be conscientious, responsible, detail-oriented, and discreet. A mystery shopper will pose as an ordinary customer and blend in with others. The shopper must note the time of arrival, do a staff and customer headcount, make a mental note of names, appearances, and remember conversations between shopper and staff.

Commitment is very important. Make sure you can do the shop within the time frame given. We all know that sometimes unexpected situations, which are out of our control, can arise.

That's why I prefer to do the shops on the first available day within the time frame given and not wait until the last day.

Once the shop is completed, there are other steps you need to follow to submit the shop. You need to adhere to correct grammar, punctuation, and spelling. You need to be a good narrator. The customer wants to experience the shop through your writing as if they were there. So being a good storyteller is a plus.

You need to make sure you can meet the submission deadline. You can do a great shop but if you miss the submission deadline you might get penalized or worst yet, not get paid for the shop. Also, shoppers are rated for their performance according to each companies guidelines, which would either increase or decrease the likelihood of you being chosen for other shops – especially the better-paying ones.

Discretion is a must. You can never disclose to anyone especially the shop staff – that you're a mystery shopper. If you blow your cover you will not get paid and can possibly harm your chances of getting any more shops for that company.

No Special Equipment Needed

You don't need any special equipment to be a mystery shopper. Chances are you already have everything to help you perform a successful shop. You will need to have a computer, a good internet connection, a cell phone with a camera and a wristwatch (cell phone can work as well). A scanner or fax will be great but it's not necessary since you can take a snapshot of receipts or materials to upload to the shop website.

Cell phones are a big asset to mystery shopping. You can discreetly text or email staff names, descriptions, and any information needed, to yourself. Also, cell phones come equipped with cameras that will certainly be necessary for most shops.

Preparing To Shop

For me to know if mystery shopping was worth my time and effort, I did various things that helped me decide. I didn't want to mix my mystery shopping expenses with my daily expenses or my earnings with my regular income. Therefore, I opened a separate checking account to use for this purpose. Nowadays you can open a checking account with $0 deposit so there is no cost involved. However, depending on the type of shops you choose, you might need to have a credit card with an available balance to do your first shops or deposit some money into the new checking account. No worries, just make sure to choose shops that will reimburse you for expenses incurred`.

Many, if not all of the companies, prefer to use PayPal for payment. Therefore, I opened a PayPal account for that purpose. Some companies will deposit directly into your checking account. And there are very few companies which will send you a check.

Getting paid varies in time depending on each company. Payments are scheduled for the 15th or the 30th of the next month after the shop and some will pay as far as 60 days later. I've shopped for very few who will pay in two weeks. Each company is different so make sure to read their agreement before signing up so you know what to expect.

Keeping Track of Your Shops

There was a time where I was doing shops almost on a daily basis for over twenty companies, and keeping track of my shops and pay was difficult. Therefore, I created a database using Excel that helped me keep track of my shops, submission dates, expenses incurred, the total of reimbursements if any, and when I got paid. Thankfully, I was never short-changed. Every company I performed a shop for paid me.

I also have a binder by month where I store the shop's reports, receipts and any supporting document that I was given during the shop. Most, if not all, shops ask that you keep the info for at least six months. Although, in my many years as a mystery shopper I have never been called months later to look over any shop done after the initial submission.

Is It Worth My Time?

It is not worth my time to do a shop that will pay me less than $30 if I need to travel more than ten miles. Therefore, I create an itinerary to follow where I pick up various shops on the route either while driving home from work or if I'm not working, one that will make my time worthwhile.

Let me explain. One of the many itineraries I choose is after work. I search for shops within all the companies I'm registered at and choose those shops that are within my route from work. For instance, I drive twenty-two miles between work and home one way. There are various grocery stores/supermarkets in the route which are featured in the companies I'm registered at. Since I work until two o'clock in the afternoon, I'm able to book at least three shops within my route. Therefore, I pack a Styrofoam cooler in my car and prepare a list of groceries to shop for keeping in mind the guidelines and requirements provided. I cannot emphasize how important it is to read the guidelines. Sometimes, a shop will need you to stay in a location for no less than 20 minutes. Therefore, a shop that is completed within less time might be missing some required steps. For a successful shop, you must be thorough.

Reliable Companies

So, what companies are out there that really do pay for mystery shopping? There are many companies looking for mystery shoppers. The list I am providing are companies that I have personally done shops for and know that they will pay you for a shop well done. And, most important of all, will NOT charge you to register with them.

These are not the only companies available. Also, you need to take in consideration that there is a bit of homework involved in registering to become a mystery shopper. The application is either short and sweet or long and tedious. Some require a narrative of personal experience, others don't.

Just a small tip: if you come across an application where you have to write a narrative, type it in a word document, save it and reuse it as needed.

You will also need to complete a Form W-9 and upload it to the company's website. No worries, this is standard in any company where you will be working as an independent contractor.

1) About Face https://aboutfacecorp.com/shopper-pathway/become-a-mystery-shopper/

2) Amusement Advantage

http://www.amusementadvantage.com/shoppers/application/

3) ATH Power Online

https://www.athpoweronline.com/index.norm.php

4) Best Mark http://www.bestmark.com/become_a_shopper.htm

5) Confero https://www.conferoinc.com/shoppers-center/become-a-shopper/

6) Coyle Hospitality

https://www.coylehospitality.com/evaluators/

7) Customer Perspectives

http://www.customerperspectives.com/shopper-registration2/

8) Game Film Consultants http://www.gamefilm-consultants.com

9) iMyst https://www.imyst.com/mysteryshopping.asp

10) Insight A Closer Look https://insight.a-closer-look.com/ShopperApplication-Start.aspx

11) Intelli-Shop https://insite.intelli-shop.com/index.norm.php

12) Jancyn http://www.jancyn.com/new-shopper-application-san-jose-ca/

13) Kern Scheduling http://kernscheduling.com/

14) Maritz CX https://www.maritzcx.com/become-a-mystery-shopper/

15) Measure CP https://measurecp.com/shoppers/

16) Mystery Shoppers Services

https://www.mysteryshopperservices.com/become-shopper/

17) National Shopping Service Network

https://www.mysteryshopper.net/shoppers

18) Premier Service https://premierservice.ca/apply/

19) Reality Based Group

http://dev1.realitybasedgroup.com/solutions/mystery-shopping-2/

20) Reality Check http://www.realitycheckservice.com/mystery-shopping/#become-a-mystery-shopper

21) Ritter Associates http://www.ritterassociates.com/become-shopper.html

22) Secret Shop https://isecretshop.com/register

23) Secret Shopper https://www.secretshopper.com/

24) Shoppers View https://shoppersview.com/

25) The Source Agents https://www.thesourceagents.com/

Where Do I Begin?

No worries, here are a few tips before you begin your application process. This in no way constitutes the order in which you should begin your venture. It is just a suggestion.

Designated E-mail

Nothing is worse than having to sort through hundreds of e-mails we receive on our personal e-mail every day looking for shop e-mails. I suggest you have a designated one exclusively for mystery shopping companies and accounts. If you don't have one you can use solely for this purpose, you might have to set it up before registering to mystery shopping companies.

Checking Account

Open a checking account, either local or online, that will be exclusively used for mystery shopping. I recommend Capital One 360 Checking. You can open it with $0 deposit and it's an online and mobile checking account and it's FREE! If you need to buy checks (not that you will be using them) they will only cost you $5.00. You can deposit checks through their mobile app. You can open your account free online at https://www.capitalone.com/bank/checking-accounts/online-checking-account/. I do not work or receive any type of compensation for recommending Capital One. I personally use this checking account and have a good experience with them.

PayPal Account

Open a PayPal account (if you don't already have one). A personal PayPal account will do just fine. It's free and easy to apply at <https://www.paypal.com/us/webapps/mpp/account-selection>. Make sure you have your bank account opened and linked to PayPal so that you can transfer your earnings to your account.

A Little Extra

To learn more about Mystery Shopping, including world-wide opportunities you can visit the Mystery Shopping Professionals Association (**MSPA**), http://www.mspa-global.org. You can register to become a member in America as an independent contractor for free. Other options are available for a fee as well. Becoming a member7 of MSPA also helps your profile to stand out for the good paying shops.

Some companies prefer that you verify your location when performing a shop. There's an app called, **GeoVerify**, for both IOS an Android phones. It's easy to use and free.

You can also download the **iSecretShop** app which will alert you to shops available in your area. You can find it in your app store for both IOS and Android phones.

Now you're ready to begin registering at your heart's content with as many shopping company's as you wish. So happy shopping everyone!

About the Author

Debbie Centeno is a part-time accountant who also runs her own bookkeeping and tax service business. She graduated Magna Cum Laude with a Bachelor's Degree in Accounting in 2012. She has been performing successful mystery shops since 2005 as a hobby. She has learned the ins and outs of mystery shopping and wanted to share it with others.

Besides accounting, Debbie enjoys writing. She has two blogs, *Traveler Wows,* www.travelerwows.com and *Debbie's Reflection,* www.debbiesreflection.com. She has self-published a book, *Diary of a Grieving Mother's Heart*, also inspired by her tragic experience and which you can find in Amazon in both, published and Kindle version.

Debbie Centeno is a Puerto Rican mother of three and wife currently living in Florida. You can contact Debbie through email at debbie413@gmail.com.

www.ingramcontent.com/pod-product-compliance
Lightning Source LLC
Chambersburg PA
CBHW071204220526
45468CB00003B/1156